Cuisinart Waffle Maker Cookbook for Beginners

*300-Day Effortless and Mouth-Watering Recipes
to Master Your Cuisinart Waffle Maker on a Budget*

Nance Girous

Table of Contents

Introduction

If you are looking for the best collection of Waffle recipes in one easy volume, then this is the book for you. If you are just trying for the first time, then this collection of the ultimate 300-Day Effortless and Mouth-Watering Recipes is all you need. Waffles are incredibly versatile and are great at making a wide range of meals - both sweet and savory. Many people don't get the most from the Cuisinart maker because they don't realize its potential.

Tasty waffles are the must-have cookbook for anyone searching for Effortless and Mouth-Watering recipes to satisfy your flavor. Instead of turning to options that might prevent complex, this book ensures that your body will continue to use it while still enjoying your favorite foods. With this recipe book, you will be able to make so many types of waffles that you won't know where to begin! But isn't it great to have so many mouth-watering Waffle recipes to choose from?

The recipes in this book are quick and easy to make and will produce some wonderful meals that will become instant family favorites that you will end up making time and time again. Get into waffling or return to waffling today and get reading now!

Chapter 1: An Overview

How to Operate

Before using your waffle maker for the first time, make sure that all packaging materials such as plastics and stickers are removed. Wipe the unit's interior and exterior to remove any dust and debris with a clean, damp cloth. Wipe with a dry paper towel afterward.

Wash and thoroughly dry the measuring cup. Remember that the unit is not water-resistant and should not be cleaned in the dishwasher nor soaked in water or any other liquids. Follow these easy steps to get you started with your new waffle maker.

1. Follow the instructions for making the batter. Once the batter is ready, plug in your unit to an electrical outlet. A red power indicator will light up, and the unit will begin to preheat for about five minutes.
2. Select your preferred waffle shade using the shade setting knob. A lower setting will yield a lighter shade and fluffier texture. The color and texture will become darker and crispier as you move up the shade settings.
3. When the blue indicator light is illuminated, the unit is ready to make waffles. You must use the measuring cup that comes with the package. Measure 160 ml of batter if you prefer a thicker waffle and 125 ml for a thinner waffle. Pour the batter at the center of the waffle plates.
4. Close the lid. The blue light will turn off and will light up again once the waffle is ready.
5. Once the blue indicator light is on, carefully open the lid and remove the waffle using silicone-tipped tongs.
6. When done cooking, gently unplug the waffle maker from the outlet and let it cool down completely before cleaning and storing.

Tips:

1. You may notice some smoke or odor when using the waffle maker for the first time. This is normal and should go away after a few more uses.
2. When making a big batch, remove any waffle pieces that are left over before pouring over fresh batter.
3. To save space, store your waffle maker vertically or upright.

4. Although a measuring cup is provided, it is not a guarantee that you will get the same result each time. Different brands and recipes will yield different batter consistencies. The key is to put a little bit less than the intended amount and adjust accordingly.

Safety Tips & Guidelines

One of the first things to do upon getting your new waffle maker is to go over the user's manual to get complete information on how to safely operate the appliance. Only those that have thoroughly read and understood the guidelines should operate and clean the unit.

Below are some of the most important things to remember when using the Cuisinar waffle maker.

1. Follow all safety precautions when using the appliance, especially when children and the elderly are present, to prevent any injuries and damage to your property.
2. To ensure the utmost safety, never let children operate the appliance alone or leave it unattended while in use.
3. Never use the appliance if you see any signs of damage, particularly to the plug and electrical cord.
4. If the appliance malfunctions, do not attempt to repair it yourself. Contact the Cuisinar customer service immediately for assistance.
5. The unit will heat up and create hot steam while in use; exercise caution to avoid any burns. Keep your face away from the appliance when opening and be careful not to touch surfaces other than the handles.
6. Place your waffle maker on a flat, stable, and heat-resistant surface that is close to a properly grounded electrical outlet in your kitchen. Use only a 120-volt AC power outlet.
7. Make sure that it is operated in a well-ventilated area and is away from table cloths, curtains, paper towels, and other flammable materials.
8. Leave ample space around the unit. Do not place it near burners, ovens, and other similar appliances that heat up.
9. Connect the cord to the unit first, before plugging it into an electrical outlet.
10. Store the electrical cord properly on the underside of the unit. Never leave it hanging or placed in such a way that it may cause tripping.

11. Keep the cord away from hot surfaces. Never yank the cord when unplugging. Instead, hold the plug firmly and remove it from the outlet.

12. Whenever possible, do not use extension cords with this appliance to avoid any accidents. If you must use an extension, make sure that the electrical rating is as great as that of the unit.

13. Never immerse or soak the unit or any of its parts in liquid to prevent electric shock. Follow the helpful tips below for the correct way of cleaning and maintaining your waffle maker.

14. The appliance is intended for use indoors and not for commercial purposes.

15. Use appropriate accessories and attachments that are recommended by the manufacturer.

16. The waffle maker is equipped with a polarized plug and is intended to be fitted in a polarized outlet only. Modifying the plug in any way may cause electric shock, fire, or injury. If you are not able to use the appliance because of this, get in touch with a skilled electrician.

Cooking Tips

1. No matter how tempting it is, never open the waffle maker if the cooking cycle is not yet completed. Doing this will break or ruin the structure of the waffle.

2. If the cycle is complete, but the waffle seems to stick. Leave it there for 30 seconds and try to open it again.

3. Aside from the indicator in the waffle maker, another way to tell if the waffle is ready is when the steam stops coming out of the appliance.

4. The waffles are best served immediately while still warm. If you must make them in advance, place the cooked waffles on a wire rack over a sheet pan to keep them crisp. You may reheat or keep them warm in an oven or toaster at 200 degrees Fahrenheit for five minutes.

5. If you prefer a crispier and a more toasted waffle, leave it on the waffle maker for longer.

6. You can make a big batch and store the rest to save time. Simply wrap completely cooled waffles in wax paper and place them in resealable bags or foil, and freeze.

7. Do not use non-stick cooking sprays on the waffle plates. You may lightly coat the plates by brushing with vegetable, grapeseed, or canola oil instead.

8. It is best to mix the batter slowly by hand when using a waffle mix. Remember not to stir the mixture too much since this will release the gases and leave your waffles flat and tough. Mix the batter only until all the lumps have dissolved. If you wish to use a hand mixer, make sure to use the low setting.

9. If you prefer your waffles to be fluffier inside, consider separating the egg whites from the yolk. You can mix the yolk with the wet ingredients. In a separate bowl, beat the egg white and sugar until it forms stiff peaks. Fold in this mixture to your batter.

10. Although the measuring cup indicates the volume for the thick and thin batter, keep in mind that different waffle mixes may provide different results as the batter thickness varies across brands. For example, cake-based waffles will produce a softer texture than regular waffle mixes.

11. If you want to put additional ingredients to your batter, add some to the measuring cup first to figure out the best ratio to use.

12. Prepare the toppings or spreads beforehand. Wash and drain the fruits or have the butter sitting at room temperature before you begin cooking waffles. You wouldn't want your perfectly cooked waffles to get cold while you prepare other ingredients.

13. The measuring cup not only helps you prevent overflows, but it is also designed to prevent any mess. You can rest the handle of the measuring cup on the side of the bowl when not in use.

14. If the batter keeps sticking to the waffle plates, you may need to add some oil or fat to your recipe.

Tips for Cleaning and Maintenance

- After each use, disconnect the unit from the outlet by gripping the plug and gently pulling away. Never yank the cord to avoid damaging the wires.

- Never try to attempt to clean the waffle maker while it is still hot. Always wait for it to completely cool or just warm enough to easily remove food but will not cause burns or injuries.

- The waffle plates are fixed to the body and cannot be taken apart for regular cleaning. They do, however, have a non-stick coating, which makes clean-up so much easier. To clean, simply remove leftover crumbs by using a soft-bristled brush or paper towel.

- Over time, you may need to also clean the exterior once it becomes grimy. Wipe the entire unit with a clean, damp cloth or paper towel.

- The waffle maker is not dishwasher-safe and should not be soaked in any form of liquid.

- Never use abrasive pads or cleaners on the waffle plates. For hard to remove food, pour some cooking oil, and let sit for five minutes until it softens. Wipe with a clean cloth or paper towel.
- Before storing, gently wrap the electrical cord underneath the unit. Make sure that you don't pull and wrap the cord too tightly as it may damage the wiring.
- Never use metal cutleries to remove food. Use silicone, wood, or rubber utensils to avoid damaging the non-stick coating.
- Before each use, inspect the cord and other parts for signs of damage or wear and tear. If cuts and abrasions are observed, do not use the appliance and contact an authorized representative.
- Keep the appliance in a cool, dry place when not in use.

Chapter 2: Savory Waffle Recipes

Potato Waffle

Preparation Time: 10 minutes
Cooking Time: 5 minutes
Servings: 2

Ingredients:

- ½ onion, chopped
- 2 potatoes, shredded
- 1 tablespoon all-purpose flour
- 2 eggs, beaten

Method:

1. Mix onion, potatoes, flour and eggs in a bowl.
2. Plug the Cuisinar Waffle Maker to preheat.
3. Pick shade that you like.
4. When you see the blue light, add the potato mixture to the machine.
5. Seal it and the blue light will turn off.
6. Wait for it to turn on again.
7. Open, let cool and serve.

Serving Suggestions: Serve topped with grilled burger patty.

Preparation & Cooking Tips: Get rid of extra moisture from potatoes.

Cornmeal Waffles with Sausage & Green Chili

Preparation Time: 10 minutes
Cooking Time: 10 minutes
Servings: 6

Ingredients:

Waffle batter

- 1 ¼ cup all-purpose flour
- ¾ cup yellow cornmeal
- 1 teaspoon baking soda
- 2 teaspoons baking powder
- 2 tablespoons sugar
- 1 teaspoon salt
- 2 eggs, beaten
- 1 ½ cups buttermilk
- ½ stick butter, melted

Sausage & green chili

- ½ lb. breakfast sausage
- ½ cup green chili, chopped
- 1 teaspoon olive oil
- 2 tablespoons flour
- 1 ¼ cups milk
- Salt and pepper to taste

Method:

1. Combine waffle batter ingredients in a bowl.
2. Mix well.
3. Plug the Cuisinar Waffle Maker to preheat.
4. Turn knob to preferred shade setting.
5. Wait for blue light to turn on before adding batter to the waffle maker.
6. Seal and blue light will turn off.
7. Wait for blue light to turn on again.
8. While waiting, cook sausage and green chili in olive oil.
9. Stir in flour and milk.
10. Season with salt and pepper.
11. Simmer for 5 minutes.
12. Pour gravy on top of waffle and serve.

Serving Suggestions: Serve with avocado slices and chopped fresh cilantro.

Preparation & Cooking Tips: Use lean turkey breakfast sausage if available.

Waffle with Bacon & Swiss Cheese

Preparation Time: 10 minutes
Cooking Time: 5 minutes
Servings: 8

Ingredients:

- 2 cups pancake mix
- 1 ½ cup milk
- 2 eggs
- 1 cup Swiss cheese, shredded
- 8 slices bacon, cooked and crumbled

Method:

1. Mix pancake mix, milk, eggs, and Swiss cheese.
2. Stir in crumbled bacon.
3. Plug the Cuisinar Waffle Maker.
4. Preheat the machine.
5. Choose preferred shade setting.
6. Add mixture to the waffle maker when blue light turns on.
7. Seal the machine (blue light will turn off).
8. Waffle is done once blue light turns on.
9. Open and serve the waffle.

Serving Suggestions: Drizzle with maple syrup or top with butter.

Preparation & Cooking Tips: You can also use Gruyere cheese in place of Swiss cheese.

Waffle Sandwich

Preparation Time: 10 minutes
Cooking Time: 15 minutes
Servings: 6

Ingredients:

Waffle

- 1 cup all-purpose flour
- 1 cup cornmeal
- ½ teaspoon baking soda
- 2 teaspoons baking powder
- 5 tablespoons butter
- 2 cups yogurt
- 2 egg yolks, beaten
- 2 egg whites, beaten
- ¼ cup maple syrup

Sandwich

- 2 slices ham
- 2 slices cheese
- 1 apple, sliced

Method:

1. Combine waffle ingredients in a bowl.
2. Plug the Cuisinar Waffle Maker to start preheating.
3. Choose desired shade setting.
4. Add batter to the waffle maker when blue light turns on.
5. Seal the waffle maker.
6. Wait for blue light to turn on again.
7. Top waffle with ham, cheese and apple.
8. Top with another waffle.
9. Bake in the oven until cheese is melted.

Serving Suggestions: Serve with Dijon mustard.

Preparation & Cooking Tips: Use plain Greek yogurt.

Ham & Gruyere Waffle

Preparation Time: 10 minutes
Cooking Time: 5 minutes
Servings: 7

Ingredients:

- 2 cups all-purpose flour
- 2 teaspoons baking powder
- ¼ cup sugar
- ½ teaspoon salt
- 2 eggs
- 5 tablespoons butter, melted
- 1 ¾ cups milk
- 6 oz. ham, diced
- 1 cup gruyere cheese, grated

Method:

1. Combine flour, baking powder, sugar and salt in a bowl.
2. In another bowl, beat together eggs, butter and milk.
3. Gradually add first bowl to the second bowl.
4. Mix well.
5. Fold in ham and cheese.
6. Plug the Cuisinar Waffle Maker to begin preheating.
7. Select preferred shade setting.
8. Once blue light is on, pour the mixture into the machine.
9. Close and wait for blue light to turn off.
10. When blue light turns on, open machine and serve waffle.

Serving Suggestions: Serve with butter or jam.

Preparation & Cooking Tips: You can also use whole wheat flour.

Poutine Waffle

Preparation Time: 10 minutes
Cooking Time: 10 minutes
Servings: 10

Ingredients:

Waffle

- 1 ½ cups flour
- ½ teaspoon baking soda
- 2 teaspoons baking powder
- 1 ½ cups buttermilk
- 2 tablespoons oil
- 1 teaspoon vanilla extract
- ½ teaspoon salt

Poutine

- 2 cups cooked French fries
- 1 cup cooked gravy
- 1 cup cheddar cheese, shredded
- 4 slices bacon, cooked crisp and crumbled

Method:

1. Mix waffle ingredients in a bowl.
2. Preheat the Cuisinar Waffle Maker.
3. Pick preferred shade setting.
4. When you see blue light is turned on, pour in the batter.
5. Close and blue light will turn off.
6. Wait for blue light to turn on as this signals that the waffle is done.
7. Top waffle with fries and gravy.
8. Sprinkle cheese and bacon on top.
9. Place waffle inside the oven and bake at 350 degrees F for 2 minutes or until cheese has melted.

Serving Suggestions: Sprinkle with a little pepper.

Preparation & Cooking Tips: Regular milk can be used in place of buttermilk.

Waffles with Cheddar & Chives

Preparation Time: 10 minutes
Cooking Time: 5 minutes
Servings: 4

Ingredients:

- 1 cup all-purpose flour
- ¼ cup cornstarch
- ½ cup yellow cornmeal
- ½ teaspoon baking soda
- 1 teaspoon baking powder
- Salt and pepper to taste
- 2 eggs, beaten
- 2 cups buttermilk
- 4 tablespoons butter, melted
- ¼ cup chives, chopped
- 3 oz. cheddar, shredded

Method:

1. Add flour, cornstarch, cornmeal, baking soda, baking powder, salt and pepper to a bowl.
2. In another bowl, mix eggs, milk and butter.
3. Add flour mixture to the egg mixture and stir well.
4. Fold in chives and cheddar.
5. Plug the Cuisinar Waffle Maker to begin preheating.
6. Turn to preferred shade setting.
7. Once blue light is on, add batter to the waffle maker.
8. Blue light will turn off when you close the machine.
9. Wait for blue light to turn on as this signals that the waffle is done.

Serving Suggestions: Sprinkle with chives.

Preparation & Cooking Tips: Use unsalted butter.

Ham & Swiss Cheese Waffle with Sunny Side Up Egg

Preparation Time: 10 minutes
Cooking Time: 5 minutes
Servings: 4

Ingredients:

- ¾ cup all-purpose flour
- 1 ½ teaspoons sugar
- 1 ½ teaspoons baking powder
- Salt and pepper to taste
- 1 egg, beaten
- ¾ cup milk
- 2 tablespoons vegetable oil
- 2 tablespoons Parmesan cheese, grated
- 2 oz. ham, diced
- ¼ cup Swiss cheese, shredded
- 4 eggs, cooked sunny side up

Method:

1. In a bowl, mix flour, sugar, baking powder, salt and pepper.
2. In another bowl, whisk together egg, milk, oil and Parmesan cheese.
3. Slowly add flour mixture to the egg mixture.
4. Fold in ham and Swiss cheese.
5. Plug the Cuisinar Waffle Maker to start preheating.
6. Select preferred shade setting.
7. Once blue light is on, add the mixture to the waffle maker.
8. Seal the machine (blue light will turn off).
9. When blue light turns on, open machine.
10. Let waffle cool and serve topped with sunny side up eggs.

Serving Suggestions: Sprinkle with chopped scallions.

Preparation & Cooking Tips: You can freeze waffles for up to 1 month. Reheat before serving.

Ricotta Waffle with Herbs

Preparation Time: 10 minutes
Cooking Time: 5 minutes
Servings: 4

Ingredients:

- 2 cups flour
- ¾ teaspoon salt
- 1 tablespoon baking powder
- 1 ¼ cups buttermilk
- 2 eggs, beaten
- ¼ cup olive oil
- ¼ cup herbs, chopped
- ½ cup ricotta cheese

Method:

1. Add all ingredients to a bowl.
2. Mix well.
3. Plug the Cuisinar Waffle Maker to start preheating.
4. Turn knob to preferred shade setting.
5. Once blue light is on, pour the mixture into the waffle maker.
6. Seal the machine.
7. Open machine when blue light turns on once more.

Serving Suggestions: Serve with chicken marsala.

Preparation & Cooking Tips: Ideal choices for the herbs are chives, rosemary, tarragon and thyme.

Cheddar & Thyme Waffle

Preparation Time: 10 minutes
Cooking Time: 5 minutes
Servings: 4

Ingredients:

- 2 eggs
- ¼ teaspoon lemon juice
- 2 ¼ cups pancake mix
- 1 tablespoon fresh thyme
- ½ teaspoon salt
- 1 cup milk
- ¼ cup vegetable oil
- 1 ½ cup cheddar cheese

Method:

1. Beat eggs in a bowl.
2. Stir in lemon juice, pancake mix and the rest of the ingredients.
3. Mix well.
4. Preheat the Cuisinar Waffle Maker by plugging the device.
5. Turn to preferred shade setting.
6. When the blue light turns on, pour in the mixture.
7. Seal and the blue light will turn off.
8. Wait for it to turn on again as this means that the waffle is done.

Serving Suggestions: Serve with breakfast sausage.

Preparation & Cooking Tips: You can also use baking mix instead of pancake mix.

Chorizo Waffle

Preparation Time: 10 minutes
Cooking Time: 5 minutes
Servings: 4

Ingredients:

- 1 ¼ cups flour
- ¾ cup cornmeal
- 1 teaspoon baking soda
- 2 teaspoon baking powder
- 2 tablespoons sugar
- 1 teaspoon salt
- 2 eggs, beaten
- 1 ½ cups buttermilk
- 4 teaspoons butter, melted
- 4 oz. chorizo, cooked
- 4 oz. cheese, grated
- 3 scallions, chopped

Method:

1. Put all the ingredients in a bowl.
2. Mix well.
3. Preheat the Cuisinar Waffle Maker.
4. Choose preferred shade setting.
5. Add batter to the waffle maker.
6. Seal the waffle maker.
7. Wait for blue light to turn on.
8. Open machine and serve waffle.

Serving Suggestions: Serve with poached eggs and chopped cilantro.

Preparation & Cooking Tips: Use extra sharp cheddar if available.

Bacon & Cheddar Waffle

Preparation Time: 10 minutes
Cooking Time: 5 minutes
Servings: 12

Ingredients:

- 2 cups pancake mix
- 1 egg, beaten
- 1 cup sour cream
- 1 cup milk
- 1 tablespoon butter, melted
- 1 cup cheddar cheese, shredded
- 6 slices bacon, cooked and chopped

Method:

1. Mix all the ingredients in a bowl, adding cheese and bacon last.
2. Plug the Cuisinar Waffle Maker to preheat.
3. Choose desired shade setting.
4. When blue light turns on, add mixture to the waffle maker.
5. Seal to turn off blue light.
6. Wait for blue light to turn to signal that the waffle is done.

Serving Suggestions: Serve with juice or fruit shake.

Preparation & Cooking Tips: You can also use turkey bacon if you want your waffles lighter.

Bacon & Cornmeal Waffle

Preparation Time: 10 minutes
Cooking Time: 5 minutes
Servings: 6

Ingredients:

- 1 ¼ cups all purpose flour
- ¾ cup yellow cornmeal
- ½ teaspoon baking soda
- 2 ¼ teaspoons baking powder
- 2 eggs, beaten
- 2 cups buttermilk
- ¼ cup butter, melted
- 3 tablespoons maple syrup
- 8 slices bacon, cooked crisp and crumbled

Method:

1. Combine all the ingredients in a bowl.
2. Plug the Cuisinar Waffle Maker to preheat.
3. Turn knob to desired shade setting.
4. Once blue light is on, add the batter into the machine.
5. Close the waffle maker.
6. Wait for blue light to turn off.
7. When blue light turns on, this means that the waffle is done.
8. Let cool and serve.

Serving Suggestions: Top with maple syrup.

Preparation & Cooking Tips: Regular milk can be used if buttermilk is not available.

Waffle with Smoked Salmon

Preparation Time: 10 minutes
Cooking Time: 5 minutes
Servings: 6

Ingredients:

- 2 cups all-purpose flour
- ½ teaspoon baking soda
- 2 teaspoons baking powder
- 5 tablespoons butter
- 2 eggs, beaten
- 1 cup cooked smoked salmon, flaked

Method:

1. In a bowl, add all the ingredients except smoked salmon.
2. Mix well.
3. Plug the Cuisinar Waffle Maker to preheat.
4. Turn knob to preferred shade setting.
5. Once blue light is on, add the batter to the waffle maker.
6. Seal the waffle maker.
7. Wait for blue light to turn on again.
8. Open and remove waffles.
9. Top with smoked salmon and serve.

Serving Suggestions: Serve with fresh green salad.

Preparation & Cooking Tips: You can also use other smoked fish for this recipe.

Waffles with Corned Beef & Egg

Preparation Time: 10 minutes
Cooking Time: 5 minutes
Servings: 6

Ingredients:

- 2 cups cooked corned beef
- 3 fried eggs

Waffles

- 2 cups all-purpose flour
- 1 teaspoons baking soda
- 2 teaspoons baking powder
- ¾ teaspoon salt
- 1 cup butter, melted
- 1 ½ cups buttermilk
- 3 eggs, beaten

Method:

1. Combine waffle ingredients in a bowl.
2. Cook in the preheated Cuisinar Waffle Maker as directed.
3. Wait for blue light to turn on again to signal that waffle is done.
4. Top waffles with corned beef and fried eggs.

Serving Suggestions: Serve with slices of cheese.

Preparation & Cooking Tips: You can also make your own corned beef if you like.

Loaded Potato WAffle

Preparation Time: 10 minutes
Cooking Time: 10 minutes
Servings: 6

Ingredients:

- 3 tablespoons all-purpose flour
- 1 teaspoon baking powder
- 2 eggs, beaten
- 2 lb. potatoes, shredded
- 1 ½ teaspoons salt
- ¾ cup cheddar cheese, shredded
- 3 tablespoons butter, melted
- ¼ cup chives, chopped
- ½ cup bacon, cooked crisp and crumbled

Method:

1. Mix all the ingredients in a bowl, adding chives and bacon last.
2. Stir well.
3. Preheat the Cuisinar Waffle Maker.
4. Pick shade setting that you prefer.
5. When the blue light is on, pour in the batter.
6. Seal the waffle maker.
7. Open only when blue light is on again.

Serving Suggestions: Serve with sour cream, additional bacon slices and melted cheese sauce.

Preparation & Cooking Tips: Be sure to squeeze potatoes dry before adding to the mixture.

Multigrain Spinach Waffle with Cheese

Preparation Time: 10 minutes

Cooking Time: 5 minutes

Servings: 4

Ingredients:

- 1 ½ cup milk
- 1 egg, beaten
- 2 tablespoons grapefruit juice
- 2 tablespoons olive oil
- 1 teaspoon vanilla extract
- ½ cup spinach puree
- 1 cup Parmesan cheese, shredded
- ½ cup whole wheat flour
- ½ cup oat flour
- ½ cup almond meal
- 2 ½ tablespoons flaxmeal
- 2 teaspoons baking powder
- Salt and pepper to taste

Method:

1. Mix milk, egg, juice, oil, vanilla, spinach and cheese in a bowl.
2. In another bowl, combine remaining ingredients.
3. Add dry mixture to the milk mixture, stirring well.
4. Plug the Cuisinar Waffle Maker to start preheating.
5. Pick your desired shade setting.
6. Wait for blue light to turn on, then pour in the batter.
7. Seal and blue light will turn off.
8. Waffle is ready when blue light turns on.
9. Let cool and serve.

Serving Suggestions: Top with sunny side up eggs.

Preparation & Cooking Tips: You can use nondairy milk such as almond milk for this recipe.

Hummus Waffles with Sausage

Preparation Time: 10 minutes

Cooking Time: 5 minutes

Servings: 6

Ingredients:

- 1 cup flour
- 1 cup whole wheat flour
- ¼ teaspoon baking soda
- 1 ½ teaspoons baking powder
- ½ teaspoon salt
- 1 cup milk
- 2 eggs, beaten
- 1 tablespoon olive oil
- ½ cup hummus
- 2 tablespoons fresh basil, chopped
- 1 sausage link, removed from casing, crumbled and cooked

Method:

1. Combine all the ingredients in a bowl.
2. Mix well.
3. Plug the Cuisinar Waffle Maker to begin preheating.
4. Select your desired shade setting.
5. Wait for blue light to turn on.
6. Once it is on, pour batter into the waffle maker.
7. Seal the machine.
8. Wait for blue light to turn on again before opening the waffle maker.
9. Let cool and serve.

Serving Suggestions: Serve with diced avocado.

Preparation & Cooking Tips: You can also add sundried tomato to the batter.

Breakfast Sandwich Waffle

Preparation Time: 10 minutes
Cooking Time: 5 minutes
Servings: 6

Ingredients:

- 10 oz. milk
- 7 oz. flour
- 3 tablespoons butter, melted
- 3 tablespoons Parmesan cheese, grated
- 1 tablespoon parsley, chopped
- 1 ½ teaspoons baking powder
- 1 egg, beaten
- 1 teaspoon sugar
- 3 teaspoons mustard
- 3 slices ham
- 3 slices cheese
- 3 sunny side up eggs

Method:

1. Add all ingredients except mustard, ham, cheese and eggs.
2. Mix well.
3. Preheat the Cuisinar Waffle Maker.
4. Pick preferred shade setting.
5. When you see blue light is turned on, pour in the batter.
6. Close and blue light will turn off.
7. Wait for blue light to turn on as this signals that the waffle is done.
8. Spread top side of waffle with mustard.
9. Top with ham, cheese and eggs.

Serving Suggestions: Sprinkle with pepper.

Preparation & Cooking Tips: Use self-rising flour if available.

Smoked Ham & Spinach Waffle

Preparation Time: 10 minutes
Cooking Time: 5 minutes
Servings: 6

Ingredients:

- 2 cups flour
- 2 teaspoons baking powder
- ¼ teaspoon baking soda
- 1 tablespoon sugar
- ½ teaspoon salt
- 1 ¾ cups milk
- 2 eggs, beaten
- ¼ cup butter, melted
- 1 cup smoked ham, diced
- 1 cup spinach puree

Method:

1. Mix all ingredients in a bowl, adding ham and spinach last.
2. Preheat Cuisinar Waffle Maker.
3. Pick the shade setting you prefer.
4. Wait for blue light to turn on.
5. Add batter to waffle maker.
6. Close.
7. Wait for blue light to turn on before opening it.
8. Let cool and serve.

Serving Suggestions: Top with scrambled eggs.

Preparation & Cooking Tips: Use regular ham if smoked ham is not available.

Waffle Club Sandwich

Preparation Time: 10 minutes
Cooking Time: 5 minutes
Servings: 6

Ingredients:

Waffle

- 2 cups flour
- 2 teaspoons baking powder
- ¼ teaspoon baking soda
- 1 tablespoon sugar
- ½ teaspoon salt
- 1 ¾ cups milk
- 2 eggs, beaten
- ¼ cup butter, melted

Club sandwich

- 4 slices ham
- 4 slices cheese
- 4 cups lettuce, chopped
- 4 eggs, cooked scrambled

Method:

1. Mix waffle ingredients in a bowl.
2. Plug the Cuisinar Waffle Maker to preheat.
3. Set to preferred shade option.
4. Wait for blue light to turn on.
5. Add mixture to the waffle maker.
6. Seal.
7. Wait for blue light to turn on once more before opening the machine.
8. Stack the waffles with the ham, cheese and lettuce in layers in between.
9. Serve.

Serving Suggestions: Serve with baked crispy potato fries.

Preparation & Cooking Tips: You can also freeze cooked waffles and reheat when ready to use.

Waffle with Sharp Cheddar & Chives

Preparation Time: 10 minutes
Cooking Time: 5 minutes
Servings: 6

Ingredients:

- 1 cup all-purpose flour
- ½ cup yellow cornmeal
- ¼ cup cornstarch
- 1 teaspoon baking powder
- ½ teaspoon baking soda
- Salt and pepper to taste
- 2 cups buttermilk
- 2 eggs, beaten
- 4 tablespoons butter, melted
- 3 oz. sharp cheddar, shredded
- ¼ cup chives, chopped

Method:

1. Mix dry ingredients in a bowl.
2. Combine wet ingredients in another bowl.
3. Add wet mixture to the first bowl and mix well.
4. Turn on the Cuisinar Waffle Maker.
5. Select shade setting that you like.
6. When the blue light is on, add mixture.
7. Close the waffle maker.
8. Wait for blue light to turn on again before opening.
9. Let cool and serve.

Serving Suggestions: Serve with deli ham slices.

Preparation & Cooking Tips: Use extra sharp cheddar cheese.

Sour Cream Waffle

Preparation Time: 10 minutes

Cooking Time: 5 minutes

Servings: 4

Ingredients:

- 2 eggs
- 1 cup buttermilk
- ¼ cup butter
- 1 cup sour cream
- 1 ½ cups all-purpose flour
- 1 teaspoon baking powder
- ½ teaspoon salt
- ¾ teaspoon baking soda

Method:

1. Beat eggs in a bowl.
2. Stir in milk, butter and sour cream.
3. Combine until smooth.
4. Gradually add the rest of the ingredients.
5. Plug Cuisinar Waffle Maker and preheat it.
6. Once blue light is on, add mixture to the waffle maker.
7. Close it.
8. Wait for blue light to turn on before opening.

Serving Suggestions: Serve with yogurt and fresh fruit slices.

Preparation & Cooking Tips: Use low-fat sour cream.

Potato Waffle with Rosemary & Garlic

Preparation Time: 10 minutes
Cooking Time: 5 minutes
Servings: 6

Ingredients:

- 1 onion, chopped
- 4 cloves garlic, minced
- 2 potatoes, shredded
- 2 eggs, beaten
- ¼ cup olive oil
- 1 cup all-purpose flour
- 2/3 cup milk
- 1 ½ teaspoons fresh rosemary, minced
- 2 teaspoons baking powder
- Salt and pepper to taste

Method:

1. Combine all the ingredients in a bowl.
2. Preheat Cuisinar Waffle Maker.
3. Choose desired shade setting.
4. Pour the mixture into the waffle maker once the blue light turns on.
5. Close it and light will turn off.
6. Wait for blue light to turn on again.
7. Open waffle maker.
8. Serve waffle.

Serving Suggestions: Serve with vegetable salad on the side.

Preparation & Cooking Tips: Use large Russet potatoes for this recipe.

Zucchini & Cheddar Waffles

Preparation Time: 10 minutes
Cooking Time: 5 minutes
Servings: 6

Ingredients:

- 2 zucchini, grated
- 1 ½ cups all purpose flour
- 2 teaspoons baking powder
- 1 tablespoon sugar
- ½ teaspoon salt
- 1 ½ cups milk
- 1 egg, beaten
- 1 cup cheddar cheese
- ½ cup yogurt

Method:

1. Squeeze zucchini to get rid of extra moisture.
2. Add to a bowl.
3. Stir in the rest of the ingredients.
4. Preheat the Cuisinar Waffle Maker.
5. Select preferred shade setting.
6. Wait for blue light to turn on before adding batter to the machine.
7. Close the waffle maker.
8. Wait for light to turn on again to signal that the waffle is done.

Serving Suggestions: Sprinkle with chopped chives.

Preparation & Cooking Tips: Use nonfat plain Greek yogurt.

Parmesan Waffle

Preparation Time: 10 minutes
Cooking Time: 5 minutes
Servings: 4

Ingredients:

- ¼ cup vegetable oil
- 1 cup buttermilk
- ¾ cup milk
- 2 eggs, beaten
- ½ teaspoon dried rosemary
- 1 teaspoon salt
- 3 teaspoons baking powder
- 1 ¾ cups all purpose flour
- ½ cup Parmesan cheese, grated

Method:

1. Put all the ingredients in a bowl.
2. Mix well.
3. Preheat your Cuisinar Waffle Maker.
4. Pick the shading you prefer.
5. Add mixture to the machine.
6. Seal and wait for cooking to be completed.

Serving Suggestions: Serve with shredded rotisserie chicken and gravy.

Preparation & Cooking Tips: To make waffle fluffier, separate egg yolk from egg white and beat egg white until stiff peaks form before adding to the mixture.

Ham Waffle with Vanilla

Preparation Time: 10 minutes
Cooking Time: 5 minutes
Servings: 6

Ingredients:

- 2 cups flour
- 3 teaspoons baking powder
- ½ teaspoon salt
- 2 teaspoons sugar
- 3 eggs, beaten
- 5 tablespoons butter, melted
- 1 ½ cups milk
- ¼ teaspoon vanilla extract
- ½ cup ham, diced

Method:

1. Add all ingredients to a bowl.
2. Mix well.
3. Turn on the Cuisinar Waffle Maker and preheat it.
4. Turn knob to preferred shade setting.
5. Add batter to machine once blue light is on.
6. Seal.
7. Wait for light to turn on again.
8. Open and serve waffle.

Serving Suggestions: Serve with sunny side up eggs.

Preparation & Cooking Tips: Use leftover ham.

Shawarma Waffle

Preparation Time: 4 hours and 15 minutes
Cooking Time: 20 minutes
Servings: 4

Ingredients:

Beef & Marinade

- 1 teaspoon salt
- 1 teaspoon all Spice
- 1 teaspoon ground cloves
- 1 teaspoon cumin
- ½ teaspoon cardamom
- ½ teaspoon cinnamon
- ½ teaspoon oregano
- ½ teaspoon paprika
- 1 lb. beef strips
- 1 tablespoon olive oil

Waffle

- 2 cups all-purpose flour
- 4 teaspoons baking powder
- 2 tablespoons sugar
- 2 eggs, beaten
- 1 ½ cups milk
- ⅓ cup butter, melted
- 1 teaspoon salt

Method:

1. Mix all spices in a bowl.
2. Add beef strips to the spice mixture.
3. Marinate for 4 hours.
4. Add olive oil to a pan over medium heat.
5. Cook beef strips in oil until browned on all sides.
6. Transfer to a plate and set aside.
7. Cook waffle in the Cuisinar Waffle Maker as directed.
8. Top waffle with shawarma and serve.

Serving Suggestions: Serve with tahini and garlic sauce.

Preparation & Cooking Tips: You can also use lamb for this recipe.

Tofu Waffle

Preparation Time: 15 minutes
Cooking Time: 5 minutes
Servings: 12

Ingredients:

- 2 egg whites, beaten
- ½ lb. soft silken tofu
- 2 ½ tablespoons vegetable oil
- 1 ½ cups milk
- ¼ teaspoon almond extract
- 2 teaspoons vanilla extract
- 1 teaspoon orange zest
- 1 cup whole wheat flour
- 1 ½ cups all-purpose flour
- 4 teaspoons baking powder
- ½ teaspoon cinnamon
- ½ teaspoon nutmeg
- ½ teaspoon salt

Method:

1. Beat egg whites until you see stiff peaks forming.
2. Stir in the rest of the ingredients.
3. Preheat the Cuisinar Waffle Maker.
4. Wait for blue light to turn on.
5. Pour mixture into the machine.
6. Close.
7. Wait for light to turn on again to signal cooking is done.

Serving Suggestions: Serve with crispy tofu fries.

Preparation & Cooking Tips: Use nonfat milk.

Waffles with Beef & Mushrooms

Preparation Time: 10 minutes
Cooking Time: 5 minutes
Servings: 6

Ingredients:

Waffle

- 2 cups all-purpose flour
- 4 teaspoons baking powder
- 2 tablespoons sugar
- 2 eggs, beaten
- 1 ½ cups milk
- ⅓ cup butter, melted
- 1 teaspoon salt

Topping

- 1 red onion, sliced into rings
- 1 cup mushrooms
- 1 tablespoon butter
- 1 lb. sirloin beef strips, cooked

Method:

1. Add waffle ingredients to a bowl.
2. Mix well.
3. Prepare in the preheated Cuisinar Waffle Maker as directed.
4. While waiting, cook onion and mushrooms in butter.
5. Top waffles with beef, onions and mushrooms.

Serving Suggestions: Serve with hot sauce.

Preparation & Cooking Tips: Use white sugar.

Herbed Waffles

Preparation Time: 10 minutes
Cooking Time: 5 minutes
Servings: 6

Ingredients:

- 2 cups all-purpose flour
- 4 teaspoons baking powder
- 2 tablespoons sugar
- 1 teaspoon salt
- 1 tablespoon thyme, chopped
- 2 tablespoons chives, chopped
- 1 tablespoon sage, chopped
- 1 tablespoon parsley, chopped
- 2 eggs, beaten
- 1 ½ cups milk
- 5 oz. butter

Method:

1. Mix the dry ingredients first, followed by the eggs, milk and butter.
2. Stir well.
3. Preheat the Cuisinar Waffle Maker.
4. Point knob to the desired shade setting.
5. Add batter to the waffle maker.
6. Seal the machine.
7. Wait for blue light to turn on before opening it.

Serving Suggestions: Serve with steamed asparagus.

Preparation & Cooking Tips: You can also use whole wheat flour.

Waffles with Poached Eggs & Mushrooms

Preparation Time: 10 minutes
Cooking Time: 5 minutes
Servings: 4

Ingredients:

Waffles

- 2 cups all-purpose flour
- 2 teaspoons baking powder
- 1 tablespoon sugar
- Salt and pepper to taste
- ¼ cup shallots, minced

- 4 tablespoons butter, melted
- 3 eggs, beaten
- 1 tablespoon rosemary, chopped
- 2 cups milk

Topping

- 1 red onion, chopped
- 3 cloves garlic, minced
- 1 ½ lb. mushrooms

- 2 tablespoons olive oil
- Salt and pepper to taste
- 8 poached eggs

Method:

1. Mix waffle ingredients in a bowl.
2. Plug in Cuisinar Waffle Maker.
3. Select shade setting by turning the knob.
4. Once blue light illuminates, add the mixture to the waffle maker.
5. Close the waffle maker.
6. Wait for blue light to turn on again.
7. Transfer waffles on a plate.
8. In a pan over medium heat, cook onion, garlic and mushrooms in olive oil.
9. Season with salt and pepper.
10. Top waffles with poached eggs and mushrooms.

Serving Suggestions: Serve with fresh green salad.

Preparation & Cooking Tips: Use buttermilk for the waffle.

Waffles with Creamy Chicken

Preparation Time: 10 minutes
Cooking Time: 20 minutes
Servings: 6

Ingredients:

- 1 tablespoon olive oil
- ½ cup onion, chopped
- 4 chicken breast fillets, sliced into cubes
- ½ carrot, sliced into cubes
- 1 cup all purpose cream
- 1 teaspoon garlic powder
- Salt and pepper to taste

Waffle

- 2 cups all-purpose flour
- 4 teaspoons baking powder
- 2 tablespoons sugar
- 2 eggs, beaten
- 1 ½ cups milk
- ⅓ cup butter, melted
- 1 teaspoon salt

Method:

1. Add oil to a pan over medium heat.
2. Cook onion for 1 minute, stirring often.
3. Add chicken and carrots.
4. Cook while stirring for 3 minutes or until chicken is fully cooked.
5. Pour in cream.
6. Season with garlic powder, salt and pepper.
7. Simmer for 5 minutes.
8. Turn off heat and set aside.
9. Add waffle ingredients to a bowl.
10. Stir well.
11. Cook in the preheated Cuisinar Waffle Maker as directed.
12. Add creamy beef on top of waffle and serve.

Serving Suggestions: Sprinkle with pepper.

Preparation & Cooking Tips: You can also add potatoes to the creamy chicken mixture.

Cheesy Beef Waffle

Preparation Time: 10 minutes
Cooking Time: 20 minutes
Servings: 7

Ingredients:

- 1 tablespoon olive oil
- 1 lb. ground beef
- Pinch garlic powder
- Salt and pepper to taste
- 2 cups flour
- ¼ cup granulated sugar
- 2 teaspoons baking powder
- ½ teaspoon salt
- 1 ¾ cups milk
- 2 eggs, beaten
- 5 tablespoons butter, melted
- 2 cups cheese sauce
- 1 cup cheddar cheese, shredded

Method:

1. Add olive oil to a pan over medium heat.
2. Cook ground beef until brown.
3. Season with garlic powder, salt and pepper.
4. Turn off heat.
5. Drain ground beef and set aside.
6. In a bowl, mix the remaining ingredients except cheese sauce and cheddar cheese.
7. Plug in the Cuisinar Waffle Maker.
8. Use the shade setting knob to choose preferred option.
9. When blue light turns on, add batter to the machine.
10. Close the waffle maker and the light will turn off.
11. Open waffle maker once blue light turns on.
12. Top waffle with cooked ground beef, cheese sauce and shredded cheddar.
13. Serve waffle.

Serving Suggestions: Sprinkle with chopped chives.

Preparation & Cooking Tips: Use lean ground beef.

Waffle with Crispy Pork Strips & Gravy

Preparation Time: 10 minutes
Cooking Time: 20 minutes
Servings: 6

Ingredients:

Waffle

- 2 cups all-purpose flour
- 4 teaspoons baking powder
- 2 eggs, beaten
- 2 tablespoons sugar
- ⅓ cup butter, melted
- 1 ½ cups milk
- 1 teaspoon salt

Pork strips & gravy

- 1 lb. pork, sliced into strips
- Salt and pepper to taste
- 1 cup breadcrumbs
- 1 cup oil
- 1 cup gravy

Method:

1. Cook waffle in the Cuisinar Waffle Maker as directed.
2. Set waffles aside on a plate.
3. Season pork strips with salt and pepper.
4. Cook in oil until golden and crispy.
5. Top waffles with pork strips.
6. Drizzle with gravy.

Serving Suggestions: Serve with mustard and hot sauce.

Preparation & Cooking Tips: You can also top gravy with crispy bacon bits.

Ranchero Waffles

Preparation Time: 30 minutes
Cooking Time: 20 minutes
Servings: 4

Ingredients:

- 2 tablespoons olive oil
- 1 cup onion, chopped
- 3 cloves garlic, crushed
- 10 oz. canned chipotle pepper in adobo sauce, minced
- 28 oz. canned crushed tomatoes
- 15 oz. canned black beans, mashed
- 1 teaspoon ground cumin
- ¼ cup cilantro, chopped

Waffles

- 1 ½ cups all-purpose flour
- 1 teaspoon baking powder
- ½ teaspoon salt
- ¾ teaspoon baking soda
- 2 eggs, beaten
- 1 cup milk
- ¼ cup butter

Method:

1. Combine waffle ingredients in a bowl.
2. Preheat Cuisinar Waffle Maker.
3. Prepare waffle as directed.
4. Set aside and prepare filling.
5. Add olive oil to a pan over medium heat.
6. Cook onion and garlic for 1 minute.
7. Stir in the remaining ingredients except cilantro.
8. Simmer for 10 minutes.
9. Turn off heat.
10. Stir in cilantro.
11. Top waffle with this mixture and serve.

Serving Suggestions: Serve with guacamole.

Preparation & Cooking Tips: You can also use buttermilk for the waffle mixture.

Smoked Ham & Manchego Waffle

Preparation Time: 10 minutes

Cooking Time: 5 minutes

Servings: 6

Ingredients:

- 1 cup yellow cornmeal
- 1 cup all purpose flour
- 2 teaspoons baking powder
- ½ teaspoon baking soda
- ¼ teaspoon salt
- 2 eggs, beaten
- ¼ cup maple syrup
- 2 cups buttermilk
- 4 tablespoons butter, melted
- 1 cup manchego cheese, shredded
- 1 cup smoked ham, diced

Method:

1. Combine cornmeal, flour, baking powder, baking soda and salt in a bowl.
2. In another bowl, mix eggs, maple syrup and buttermilk.
3. Add flour mixture to the egg mixture.
4. Mix well.
5. Fold in cheese and ham.
6. Preheat Cuisinar Waffle Maker.
7. Pour batter into waffle machine when blue light is on.
8. Seal the machine.
9. Wait for blue light to turn on again.
10. Open and serve waffle.

Serving Suggestions: Serve with butter.

Preparation & Cooking Tips: Shake buttermilk before using.

Waffle Nachos

Preparation Time: 15 minutes
Cooking Time: 5 minutes
Servings: 6

Ingredients:

Waffle

- 2 cups all-purpose flour
- 4 teaspoons baking powder
- 1 teaspoon salt
- 1 ½ cups milk
- 2 eggs
- ¼ cup butter, melted
- 1 teaspoon vanilla extract

Toppings

- 2 tomatoes, chopped
- 10 slices bacon, cooked crisp and crumbled
- 6 oz. black olives, sliced
- 3 green onions, chopped
- 1 ½ cups Monterey Jack cheese, shredded
- 1 ½ cups cheddar cheese, shredded

Method:

1. Mix waffle ingredients in a bowl.
2. Preheat the Cuisinar Waffle Maker.
3. Pick shade setting that you like.
4. Once blue light is on, pour mixture into the waffle maker.
5. Seal the machine.
6. Open waffle maker when blue light turns on.
7. Remove waffles.
8. Arrange waffles on a plate.
9. Add the toppings on top of the waffles.

Serving Suggestions: Serve with salsa and guacamole.

Preparation & Cooking Tips: You can also add cooked ground beef as toppings.

Waffle with Bacon, Cheese & Crispy Chicken

Preparation Time: 10 minutes
Cooking Time: 5 minutes
Servings: 6

Ingredients:

Waffle

- 2 cups all-purpose flour
- 1 teaspoon baking powder
- ½ teaspoon baking soda
- 1 ½ teaspoons salt
- 2 tablespoons sugar
- 2 cups buttermilk
- 3 eggs, beaten
- 2 tablespoons butter, melted

Filling

- 6 slices bacon, cooked crisp
- 12 breaded chicken strips, cooked crisp
- 6 oz. cheddar cheese, grated

Method:

1. Combine waffle ingredients in a bowl.
2. Mix well.
3. Preheat the Cuisinar Waffle Maker.
4. Choose shade setting that you like.
5. Once blue light is on, add mixture.
6. Seal the waffle maker.
7. Wait for blue light to turn on again.
8. Open and transfer waffle to a plate.
9. Top 3 waffles with filling ingredients.
10. Top with the other 3 waffles and serve.

Serving Suggestions: Serve with ketchup and mustard.

Preparation & Cooking Tips: You can also use mozzarella cheese for this recipe.

Waffle with Kimchi & Cheese

Preparation Time: 10 minutes
Cooking Time: 5 minutes
Servings: 4

Ingredients:

- 2 cups all-purpose flour
- 1 teaspoons baking soda
- 2 teaspoons baking powder
- ¾ teaspoon salt
- 1 cup butter, melted
- 1 ½ cups buttermilk
- 3 eggs, beaten
- 1 cup cheddar cheese, grated
- 1 cup kimchi, chopped
- 3 scallions, chopped
- 2 chili peppers, chopped

Method:

1. Combine all the ingredients in a bowl.
2. Preheat the Cuisinar Waffle Maker.
3. Pick shade setting by turning the knob.
4. Once blue light illuminates, pour batter into the machine.
5. Seal and wait for blue light to turn on again.
6. Serve waffles on a plate.

Serving Suggestions: Serve with additional kimchi.

Preparation & Cooking Tips: Squeeze kimchi dry before preparing.

Chapter 3: Sweet Waffle Recipes

Hawaiian Waffle

Preparation Time: 10 minutes
Cooking Time: 5 minutes
Servings: 6

Ingredients:

Syrup

- ¼ cup pineapple juice
- 20 oz. canned crushed pineapple
- ½ cup corn syrup
- ½ cup coconut flakes
- ½ cup sugar

Waffle

- 2 cups all-purpose flour
- 4 teaspoons baking powder
- 1 tablespoon sugar
- ½ teaspoon salt
- 2 eggs
- 1 cup milk
- ¼ cup butter, melted
- 8 oz. canned crushed pineapple
- ¼ cup coconut flakes

Method:

1. Add syrup ingredients to a pan over medium heat.
2. Bring to a boil.
3. Simmer for 15 minutes.
4. Transfer to a bowl and set aside.
5. In a bowl, combine waffle ingredients.
6. Mix well.
7. Prepare waffle in the Cuisinar Waffle Maker, following the manufacturer's instructions.
8. Drizzle with syrup and serve.

Serving Suggestions: Serve top with nuts.

Preparation & Cooking Tips: Use light corn syrup.

Apple & Caramel Waffle

Preparation Time: 10 minutes
Cooking Time: 5 minutes
Servings: 4

Ingredients:

Waffle

- 1 ¼ cups flour
- 2 teaspoons baking powder
- 1 tablespoon white sugar
- 1 teaspoon cinnamon
- ½ teaspoon salt
- 1 cup milk
- 1 egg, beaten
- 1 teaspoon vanilla extract
- 3 tablespoons oil

Sauce

- 1/3 cup water
- 1 ¼ cup brown sugar
- 4 tablespoons butter
- 1 teaspoon vanilla extract
- ½ cup whipping cream

Apples

- 3 apples, sliced thinly
- 2 tablespoons butter
- 2 tablespoons brown sugar
- 1 teaspoon cinnamon
- ¼ teaspoon nutmeg

Method:

1. Combine waffle ingredients in a bowl.
2. Prepare in the Cuisinar Waffle Maker as directed.
3. While waiting, prepare the sauce by adding water and sugar to a pot over medium heat.
4. Bring to a boil.
5. Reduce heat and simmer for 5 minutes.
6. Stir in the butter.
7. Cook for 2 minutes.
8. Turn off heat.
9. Add vanilla and cream to mixture. Set aside.

10. In a pan over medium heat, add apples and the rest of the ingredients.
11. Cook while stirring for 5 minutes.
12. Assemble the waffles by topping the waffles with the apples and drizzling with sauce.

Serving Suggestions: Serve immediately.

Preparation & Cooking Tips: Use canola oil for the waffle.

Pecan Waffle

Preparation Time: 10 minutes
Cooking Time: 5 minutes
Servings: 6

Ingredients:

- 1 ¼ cups all-purpose flour
- ¼ cup wheat bran
- 2 ½ teaspoons baking powder
- 1 tablespoon sugar
- ½ teaspoon salt
- 2 eggs
- 2 tablespoons canola oil
- 1 ½ cups milk
- 1/3 cup pecans, chopped

Method:

1. Combine flour, wheat bran, baking powder, sugar and salt in a bowl.
2. In another bowl, beat eggs and stir in oil and milk.
3. Add this to the flour mixture and mix well.
4. Fold in pecans.
5. Preheat the Cuisinar Waffle Maker.
6. Bake in the waffle maker as directed.

Serving Suggestions: Top with cream and sprinkle with pecans.

Preparation & Cooking Tips: Use nonfat milk.

Sweet Potato Waffle

Preparation Time: 10 minutes
Cooking Time: 5 minutes
Servings: 6

Ingredients:

- 1 ½ cups all-purpose flour
- ½ teaspoon baking powder
- ½ teaspoon baking soda
- 1 cup sweet potato puree
- ½ teaspoon ground cinnamon
- ¼ teaspoon salt
- 2 eggs
- 1/3 cup vegetable oil
- ¾ cup buttermilk
- 3 tablespoons brown sugar

Method:

1. Mix all the ingredients in a bowl.
2. Plug the Cuisinar Waffle Maker.
3. Pick preferred shade option.
4. When you see the blue light turn on, add the batter to the waffle maker.
5. Close and light will turn off.
6. Waffle is ready when blue light turns on again.

Serving Suggestions: Serve with maple syrup and sprinkle with mini marshmallows.

Preparation & Cooking Tips: Use homemade pureed sweet potatoes.

Black Forrest Waffle

Preparation Time: 10 minutes
Cooking Time: 5 minutes
Servings: 6

Ingredients:

- 1 ¾ cup cake flour
- 1 tablespoon baking powder
- 1/3 cup sugar
- ½ teaspoon salt
- 2 eggs
- ½ teaspoon vanilla
- ¼ cup butter
- 1 cup milk
- 2 oz. chocolate chips

Method:

1. In a bowl, mix cake flour, baking powder, sugar and salt.
2. In another bowl, beat the eggs.
3. Stir vanilla, butter and milk.
4. Add this to the first bowl.
5. Mix well.
6. Fold in chocolate chips.
7. Bake in the Cuisinar Waffle Maker as directed.

Serving Suggestions: Top waffle with pie filling or fruit jam.

Preparation & Cooking Tips: You can also use all purpose flour in place of cake flour.

Banana & Cinnamon Waffle

Preparation Time: 10 minutes
Cooking Time: 5 minutes
Servings: 4

Ingredients:

- 2 cups all-purpose flour
- 1 teaspoon baking powder
- 1 teaspoon cinnamon
- ¼ teaspoon salt
- 2 eggs, beaten
- 1 ½ cups milk
- 5 tablespoons butter, melted
- 2 bananas, mashed
- ½ cup applesauce

Method:

1. Add flour, baking powder, cinnamon and salt to a bowl.
2. Stir in eggs, milk and butter.
3. Fold in bananas and applesauce.
4. Mix well.
5. Prepare waffle in the Cuisinar Waffle Maker according to directions.

Serving Suggestions: Drizzle with honey and top with banana slices.

Preparation & Cooking Tips: Use very ripe bananas.

Waffle with Cinnamon Cream Syrup

Preparation Time: 10 minutes

Cooking Time: 5 minutes

Servings: 6

Ingredients:

- 2 cups all-purpose flour
- 2 teaspoons baking powder
- ½ teaspoon salt
- 1 tablespoon sugar
- 2 cups milk
- 3 eggs, beaten
- ¼ cup canola oil

Syrup

- ¼ cup water
- 1 cup sugar
- ½ cup corn syrup
- 1 teaspoon vanilla extract
- 5 oz. evaporated milk
- ½ teaspoon ground cinnamon

Method:

1. Add flour, baking powder, salt and sugar to a bowl and stir.
2. Beat in the milk, eggs and oil.
3. Mix well.
4. Bake in the Cuisinar Waffle Maker as directed.
5. In a pan over medium heat, combine syrup ingredients.
6. Bring to a boil and then simmer for 2 minutes.
7. Pour syrup over waffle and serve.

Serving Suggestions: Top with mixed berries.

Preparation & Cooking Tips: You can also freeze waffle and simply reheat when ready to serve.

Pumpkin Waffle with Orange & Walnut

Preparation Time: 10 minutes

Cooking Time: 5 minutes

Servings: 4

Ingredients:

- ½ cup butter
- ¼ cup walnuts, chopped
- 1 tablespoon orange zest

Waffle

- 1 cup all-purpose flour
- ¼ teaspoon baking soda
- ½ teaspoon baking powder
- 2 tablespoons brown sugar
- 1 teaspoon ground cinnamon
- ½ teaspoon salt
- 1 cup milk
- 2 eggs
- 2 tablespoons butter, melted
- ½ cup pureed pumpkin

Method:

1. In a pan over medium heat, add butter to melt.
2. Stir in walnuts and orange zest.
3. Turn off heat and set aside.
4. In a bowl, mix flour, baking soda, baking powder, sugar, cinnamon and salt.
5. In another bowl, whisk together remaining ingredients.
6. Combine two bowls.
7. Prepare waffles as directed.
8. Serve with orange mixture.

Serving Suggestions: Drizzle with maple syrup.

Preparation & Cooking Tips: Use toasted walnuts.

Lemon & Blueberry Waffle

Preparation Time: 10 minutes
Cooking Time: 5 minutes
Servings: 7

Ingredients:

- 2 cups all-purpose flour
- 1 teaspoon baking soda
- 1/3 cup granulated sugar
- ¼ teaspoon salt
- 3 eggs, beaten
- 1 tablespoon lemon juice
- 1 teaspoon lemon zest
- 2 cups buttermilk
- ½ teaspoon vanilla extract
- 4 tablespoons butter, melted
- 1 cup blueberries

Method:

1. In a bowl, mix flour, baking soda, sugar and salt.
2. In another bowl, combine rest of the ingredients except blueberries.
3. Add first bowl to the second one.
4. Mix well.
5. Stir in blueberries.
6. Plug the Cuisinar Waffle Maker.
7. Turn shade setting knob to set your preference.
8. When you see the blue light turn on, add batter.
9. Seal machine and blue light will turn off.
10. Wait for it to turn on again.
11. Open waffle maker and serve waffle.

Serving Suggestions: Serve with honey or maple syrup.

Preparation & Cooking Tips: Use freshly squeezed lemon juice and freshly grated lemon zest.

Lemon Waffle

Preparation Time: 10 minutes
Cooking Time: 5 minutes
Servings: 4

Ingredients:

- 1 ¼ cups flour
- ¼ cup sugar
- ½ teaspoon baking powder
- ½ teaspoon salt
- 1 cup milk
- ¼ cup butter, melted
- 4 eggs
- 1 tablespoon lemon juice
- 1 teaspoon lemon zest

Method:

1. Mix flour, sugar, baking powder and salt in a bowl.
2. Stir in milk, butter, eggs, lemon juice and lemon zest.
3. Preheat Cuisinar Waffle Maker.
4. Choose shade setting that you prefer.
5. Add batter when you see blue light turn on.
6. Seal and blue light will turn off.
7. Waffle is ready when blue light turns on again.

Serving Suggestions: Serve with maple syrup.

Preparation & Cooking Tips: Use freshly squeezed lemon juice and freshly grated lemon zest.

Gingerbread Waffle

Preparation Time: 20 minutes
Cooking Time: 5 minutes
Servings: 6

Ingredients:

Icing

- 2 oz. cream cheese, softened
- ½ cup butter, melted
- 1 ½ cups sugar
- ½ teaspoon vanilla extract
- 2 tablespoons milk
- 1/8 teaspoon salt

Waffle

- 2 cups all-purpose flour
- ¼ cup brown sugar
- 1 ½ teaspoons ground ginger
- 3 teaspoons baking powder
- 1 teaspoon baking soda
- 1 teaspoon ground cinnamon
- ¼ teaspoon ground nutmeg
- ½ teaspoon salt
- 2 cups buttermilk
- 4 eggs
- ½ cup butter, melted
- ½ cup molasses
- 2 teaspoons vanilla extract

Method:

1. Combine icing ingredients.
2. Mix with a hand mixer until fluffy. Set aside.
3. Combine waffle ingredients mixing dry ingredients first and then stirring in wet ingredients.
4. Prepare in the Cuisinar Waffle Maker as directed.
5. Top waffle with icing and serve.

Serving Suggestions: Serve with syrup of choice.

Preparation & Cooking Tips: You can also freeze waffles and reheat when ready to serve.

Strawberry & Grapefruit Waffle

Preparation Time: 15 minutes
Cooking Time: 15 minutes
Servings: 4

Ingredients:

Waffle

- 1 cup all-purpose flour
- 1 cup milk
- 2 eggs, beaten
- 2 tablespoons sugar
- 1 tablespoon canola oil
- 2 teaspoons baking powder
- 2 teaspoons cinnamon
- 1 teaspoon grapefruit zest

Topping

- ¼ cup grapefruit juice
- ¼ cup honey
- ¾ cup strawberries, sliced

Method:

1. Add all waffle ingredients to a food processor.
2. Pulse until smooth.
3. Let batter sit for 5 minutes.
4. Preheat the Cuisinar Waffle Maker.
5. Choose shade setting.
6. Once blue light is on, pour in the batter.
7. Close and wait for baking to complete.
8. In a pan over medium heat, simmer juice, honey and strawberries for 10 minutes.
9. Pour sauce over the waffle and serve.

Serving Suggestions: Serve topped with grapefruit segments. Dust with powdered sugar.

Preparation & Cooking Tips: Use pink grapefruit juice.

Buttermilk Waffle

Preparation Time: 10 minutes
Cooking Time: 5 minutes
Servings: 6

Ingredients:

- 1 ¾ cups all-purpose flour
- 1 teaspoon baking soda
- 1 teaspoon baking powder
- ½ teaspoon salt
- 2 cups buttermilk
- 1/3 cup canola oil
- 2 eggs

Method:

1. Mix flour, baking soda, baking powder and salt in a bowl.
2. Stir in milk, oil and eggs.
3. Follow directions for cooking waffle in the Cuisinar Waffle Maker.

Serving Suggestions: Top with whipped cream and sliced strawberries.

Preparation & Cooking Tips: Use low-fat buttermilk.

Peaches & Cream Waffle

Preparation Time: 10 minutes
Cooking Time: 5 minutes
Servings: 6

Ingredients:

- 1 cup all-purpose flour
- 1 teaspoon baking powder
- 1 tablespoon sugar
- ¼ teaspoon salt
- 2 eggs
- 1 cup milk
- ¼ teaspoon vanilla extract
- 2 tablespoons butter, melted
- 1 ¼ cups peaches, chopped
- 2 cups whipped cream
- ¾ cup peach yogurt

Method:

1. Mix flour, baking powder, sugar and salt in a bowl.
2. In another, beat eggs and milk.
3. Stir in vanilla and butter.
4. Add flour mixture to the second bowl. Mix well.
5. Fold in peaches.
6. Prepare waffles in the Cuisinar Waffle Maker as directed.
7. While waiting, beat whipped cream and yogurt in another bowl with a mixer until light and fluffy.
8. Top waffle with cream.

Serving Suggestions: Sprinkle with toasted pecans.

Preparation & Cooking Tips: Use sweetened whipped cream.

Oatmeal Waffle

Preparation Time: 10 minutes
Cooking Time: 5 minutes
Servings: 6

Ingredients:

- 1 cup oats
- 1 ½ cups all-purpose flour
- ½ teaspoon ground cinnamon
- 3 teaspoons baking powder
- ¼ teaspoon salt
- 2 eggs
- 6 tablespoons butter, melted
- 2 tablespoons brown sugar
- 1 ½ cups milk

Method:

1. Mix oats, flour, cinnamon, baking powder and salt in a bowl.
2. In another bowl, beat the eggs.
3. Stir in butter, sugar and milk.
4. Add this to the flour mixture and mix well.
5. Preheat the Cuisinar Waffle Maker.
6. Pick preferred shade setting.
7. Once blue light is on, add batter.
8. Seal and wait for baking to be completed.

Serving Suggestions: Serve with fresh fruits and yogurt.

Preparation & Cooking Tips: Use quick-cooking if available.

Maple & Walnut Waffle

Preparation Time: 10 minutes
Cooking Time: 5 minutes
Servings: 6

Ingredients:

- 2 cups all-purpose flour
- ½ teaspoon baking soda
- 1 ½ teaspoons baking powder
- ¼ teaspoon salt
- 1 ½ cups buttermilk
- 2 eggs, beaten
- 1/3 cup oil
- ½ cup maple syrup
- ½ cup walnuts, chopped

Method:

1. Combine all the ingredients in a bowl, adding walnuts last.
2. Preheat the Cuisinar Waffle Maker.
3. Follow the directions for preparing the waffle.
4. Serve immediately.

Serving Suggestions: Drizzle with maple syrup.

Preparation & Cooking Tips: Toast walnuts first before adding to the mixture.

Almond & Vanilla Waffle

Preparation Time: 10 minutes
Cooking Time: 5 minutes
Servings: 6

Ingredients:

- 5 tablespoons butter, melted
- 1 ½ cups self-rising flour
- 1 tablespoon sugar
- 2 eggs, beaten
- 1 ½ cups milk
- 1 teaspoon vanilla flavoring
- ½ teaspoon almond flavoring

Method:

1. Mix all the ingredients in a bowl.
2. Prepare waffle according to Cuisinar Waffle Maker instructions.
3. Let cool and serve.

Serving Suggestions: Serve with toffee sauce.

Preparation & Cooking Tips: Use all-purpose flour is self-rising flour is not available.

Dessert Waffle

Preparation Time: 15 minutes
Cooking Time: 15 minutes
Servings: 6

Ingredients:

Waffle

- 2 ½ cups flour
- 2 teaspoons baking powder
- ½ teaspoon salt
- 6 tablespoons brown sugar
- 2 cups cream
- 4 eggs, beaten
- ¼ cup butter, melted

Sauce

- ½ cup sugar
- 2 tablespoons of sherry wine
- 1 cup strawberries

Method:

1. Mix waffle ingredients to a bowl.
2. Prepare waffle according to Cuisinar Waffle Maker.
3. Add sauce ingredients to a pan over medium heat.
4. Simmer for 10 minutes.
5. Pour sauce over waffle and serve.

Serving Suggestions: Serve with fresh fruit slices.

Preparation & Cooking Tips: You can also add chopped nuts to the mixture.

Cranberry & Pumpkin Waffle

Preparation Time: 1 hour and 10 minutes
Cooking Time: 5 minutes
Servings: 4

Ingredients:

- ½ cup dried cranberries
- 2 cups all-purpose flour
- 2 tablespoons sugar
- 4 teaspoons baking powder
- 1 teaspoon ground ginger
- 1 teaspoon ground cinnamon
- 1 teaspoon salt
- 2 eggs, beaten
- 1 ½ cups milk
- ¼ cup solid vegetable shortening
- 1 cup pureed pumpkin
- 4 tablespoons butter

Method:

1. Soak cranberries in water for 1 hour and then drain.
2. In a bowl, add flour, sugar, baking powder, spices and salt. Stir.
3. In another bowl, beat eggs, milk, shortening, pumpkin and butter.
4. Add flour mixture to the egg mixture.
5. Fold in cranberries.
6. Prepare waffle in the Cuisinar Waffle Maker as directed.
7. Let cool and serve.

Serving Suggestions: Drizzle with syrup before serving.

Preparation & Cooking Tips: Use pumpkin puree or make your own.

Cashew Waffle

Preparation Time: 10 minutes
Cooking Time: 5 minutes
Servings: 6

Ingredients:

- 1 cup cashews
- 2 tablespoons coconut flour
- ¾ teaspoon baking soda
- ¼ teaspoon salt
- 2 eggs
- 2 tablespoons honey
- 3 tablespoons oil
- 1/4 cup water

Method:

1. Put all the ingredients in a food processor.
2. Process until smooth.
3. Preheat the Cuisinar Waffle Maker.
4. Turn knob to preferred shade setting.
5. Add batter to the machine once blue light is on.
6. Close it and light will turn off.
7. Wait for light to turn on again as this signals waffle is done.

Serving Suggestions: Serve with fresh fruits.

Preparation & Cooking Tips: If coconut flour is not available, use all-purpose flour.

Chocolate Brownie Waffle

Preparation Time: 10 minutes
Cooking Time: 5 minutes
Servings: 6

Ingredients:

- 1 ¾ cups pancake mix
- 3 tablespoons cocoa
- ¼ cup chocolate chips
- 1/3 cup walnuts, chopped
- 3 tablespoons sugar
- 1 egg, beaten
- 1 ¼ cups water
- ¼ cup vegetable oil

Method:

1. Add all the ingredients to a bowl.
2. Mix well.
3. Prepare the waffle according to the manufacturer's directions.
4. Serve immediately.

Serving Suggestions: Top with whipped cream.

Preparation & Cooking Tips: Use semi-sweet chocolate chips.

Chocolate Chip Waffle

Preparation Time: 10 minutes
Cooking Time: 5 minutes
Servings: 6

Ingredients:

- 1 ¾ all-purpose cups flour
- 2 teaspoons baking powder
- 1 tablespoon sugar
- ½ teaspoon salt
- 3 egg yolks
- 3 egg whites, beaten until light
- ½ cup vegetable oil
- 1 ¾ cups milk
- 2 cups chocolate chips

Method:

1. Add flour, baking powder, sugar and salt to a bowl. Mix well.
2. In another bowl, whisk together egg yolks, egg whites, oil and milk.
3. Add this to the first bowl, and stir.
4. Fold in chocolate chips.
5. Bake waffle in the Cuisinar Waffle Maker as directed.

Serving Suggestions: Drizzle with chocolate syrup.

Preparation & Cooking Tips: Use dark chocolate chips.

Waffle with Berries

Preparation Time: 10 minutes
Cooking Time: 5 minutes
Servings: 6

Ingredients:

Waffle

- 2 cups all-purpose flour
- 4 teaspoons baking powder
- 2 tablespoons sugar
- 2 eggs, beaten
- 1 ½ cups milk
- 4 tablespoons butter

Topping

- 2 tablespoons blackberry jam
- ¼ cup strawberries, diced
- ¼ cup blackberries, diced

Method:

1. Combine waffle ingredients in a bowl.
2. Mix well.
3. Plug the Cuisinar Waffle Maker to start preheating.
4. Choose shade setting.
5. Wait for blue light to turn on before pouring in the batter.
6. Close and cook.
7. When blue light turns on again, open the machine.
8. Serve the waffle.

Serving Suggestions: Serve with vanilla ice cream.

Preparation & Cooking Tips: Use fresh fruits not frozen for this recipe.

Oatmeal & Pecan Waffle

Preparation Time: 10 minutes

Cooking Time: 5 minutes

Servings: 8

Ingredients:

- 1 cup rolled oats
- 1 cup whole wheat flour
- ½ cup all-purpose flour
- 2 teaspoons baking powder
- ½ teaspoon salt
- 2 eggs, beaten
- 2 cups milk
- ¼ cup butter, melted
- 2 tablespoons honey
- 1 cup pecans, chopped

Method:

1. Add oats to a food processor.
2. Pulse until finely ground.
3. Transfer oats to a bowl.
4. Stir in the rest of the ingredients.
5. Prepare waffle in the Cuisinar Waffle Maker as directed.

Serving Suggestions: Serve with chocolate syrup.

Preparation & Cooking Tips: Walnuts can also be used for this recipe.

Blueberry Waffle

Preparation Time: 10 minutes
Cooking Time: 5 minutes
Servings: 6

Ingredients:

- 2 eggs
- 1 1/3 cups milk
- 1 teaspoon vanilla
- 1/3 cup butter, melted
- 2 cups all-purpose flour
- 2 teaspoons baking powder
- 2 tablespoons sugar
- ¾ teaspoon cinnamon
- Pinch salt
- 1 cup blueberries

Method:

1. Beat eggs in a bowl.
2. Stir in milk, vanilla and butter.
3. Gradually add dry ingredients, folding in blueberries last.
4. Prepare waffle in the Cuisinar Waffle Maker following the instructions of the manufacturer.

Serving Suggestions: Serve with blueberry slices.

Preparation & Cooking Tips: If using frozen waffle, thaw and drain excess water.

Apple & Cinnamon Waffle

Preparation Time: 10 minutes
Cooking Time: 5 minutes
Servings: 6

Ingredients:

- 2 cups all-purpose flour
- 3 tablespoons sugar
- 2 teaspoons baking powder
- ½ teaspoon salt
- 2 eggs
- 2 teaspoons cinnamon
- 1 ¼ cups milk
- 1/3 cup vegetable oil
- 1 apple, chopped

Method:

1. Combine all the ingredients in a bowl, adding apples last.
2. Bake in the Cuisinar Waffle Maker as directed.
3. Let cool and serve.

Serving Suggestions: Drizzle with maple syrup.

Preparation & Cooking Tips: You can also slice the apple thinly instead of chop it.

Peach, Lemon & Vanilla Waffle

Preparation Time: 10 minutes
Cooking Time: 5 minutes
Servings: 6

Ingredients:

- 2 cups all-purpose flour
- 2 teaspoons baking powder
- ½ cup sugar
- 1/3 cup butter
- ½ teaspoon salt
- 2 eggs
- 1 cup milk
- ½ teaspoon lemon juice
- ½ teaspoon vanilla
- 2 cups peaches, chopped

Method:

1. Mix dry ingredients in a bowl.
2. Stir in eggs, milk, lemon juice and vanilla.
3. Fold in peaches.
4. Prepare waffle according to Cuisinar Waffle Maker procedure.
5. Let cool and serve.

Serving Suggestions: Top with peach syrup, peach slices and whipped cream.

Preparation & Cooking Tips: Use freshly squeezed lemon juice.

Peanut Butter & Jelly Waffle Sandwich

Preparation Time: 15 minutes
Cooking Time: 5 minutes
Servings: 4

Ingredients:

Waffle

- 1 ¼ cup all-purpose flour
- 1 tablespoon baking powder
- ¼ teaspoon baking soda
- 2 tablespoons sugar
- ¼ teaspoon salt
- 1 ¼ cup milk
- 5 tablespoons peanut butter
- 2 eggs, beaten
- 3 tablespoons butter

Filling

- Fruit jelly
- Peanut butter

Method:

1. Add all the waffle ingredients to a bowl.
2. Mix well.
3. Prepare waffle in the Cuisinar Waffle Maker as directed.
4. Spread fruit jelly and peanut butter on one side of the waffle.
5. Stack with another waffle to create the sandwich.

Serving Suggestions: Let cool, slice in half and serve.

Preparation & Cooking Tips: You can also use almond milk instead of dairy milk.

Multi-Grain Apple Waffle

Preparation Time: 15 minutes
Cooking Time: 5 minutes
Servings: 6

Ingredients:

- ¼ cup cornmeal
- ¼ cup buckwheat flour
- ½ cup whole wheat flour
- ½ teaspoon baking powder
- ½ teaspoon baking soda
- ¼ teaspoon salt
- ½ cup yogurt
- 2 eggs, beaten
- 2 tablespoons water
- 1 teaspoon vanilla extract
- 1 tablespoon canola oil
- 1 cup apple, chopped

Method:

1. Mix all the ingredients in a bowl, adding apples last.
2. Bake in the Cuisinar Waffle Maker as directed.
3. Let cool and serve.

Serving Suggestions: Serve with syrup of choice.

Preparation & Cooking Tips: Use plain Greek yogurt.

Applesauce Waffle

Preparation Time: 10 minutes
Cooking Time: 5 minutes
Servings: 6

Ingredients:

- 2 cups all-purpose flour
- 2 teaspoons baking powder
- ½ cup sugar
- ¼ teaspoon ground nutmeg
- 1/8 teaspoon ground cloves
- ½ teaspoon cinnamon
- ¼ teaspoon salt
- 1 cup milk
- 3 eggs, beaten
- 1 teaspoon vanilla
- ½ cup applesauce
- 4 tablespoons butter, melted

Method:

1. Combine flour, baking powder, sugar, nutmeg, cloves, cinnamon and salt in a bowl.
2. In another bowl, stir in the remaining ingredients.
3. Add egg mixture to the flour mixture. Mix well.
4. Prepare waffle according to Cuisinar Waffle Maker instructions.
5. Let cool and serve.

Serving Suggestions: Spread butter on top of waffle and top with fresh fruit slices.

Preparation & Cooking Tips: You can also use nondairy milk such as almond milk for this recipe.

Coconut Waffle

Preparation Time: 10 minutes
Cooking Time: 5 minutes
Servings: 6

Ingredients:

- 1 ½ cups all-purpose flour
- 2 teaspoons baking powder
- ½ cup coconut flakes
- 2 tablespoons honey
- 2 tablespoons maple syrup
- 3 large eggs - separated
- 2/3 cup milk
- 1 teaspoon vanilla extract
- 1/4 cup canola oil

Method:

1. Mix dry ingredients in a bowl.
2. Gradually add wet ingredients to the flour mixture.
3. Mix well.
4. Preheat the Cuisinar Waffle Maker.
5. Pour the mixture into the waffle maker once blue light is on.
6. Seal and blue light will turn off.
7. Wait for blue light to turn on.

Serving Suggestions: Top with coconut flakes.

Preparation & Cooking Tips: Use reduced fat milk.

Carrot Cake Waffle

Preparation Time: 10 minutes
Cooking Time: 5 minutes
Servings: 6

Ingredients:

- 1 box carrot cake mix
- ½ cup walnuts, chopped
- ½ cup water
- 2 tablespoons butter
- 1 tablespoon lemon juice

Method:

1. Mix all the ingredients in a bowl.
2. Preheat the Cuisinar Waffle Maker.
3. Select preferred shade option.
4. Once blue light is on, add the batter to the machine.
5. Close and blue light will turn off.
6. Waffle is ready when blue light turns on again.

Serving Suggestions: Serve with sour cream.

Preparation & Cooking Tips: You can also use pecans if walnuts are not available.

Cinnamon French Toast Waffle

Preparation Time: 30 minutes
Cooking Time: 5 minutes
Servings: 4

Ingredients:

- 8 slices bread
- 4 eggs
- 1 cup milk
- 1 teaspoon vanilla
- ¾ teaspoon cinnamon
- 1 tablespoon sugar
- ¼ teaspoon salt

Method:

1. Slice bread into cubes.
2. In a bowl, mix the remaining ingredients.
3. Soak the bread in the mixture for 15 minutes.
4. Preheat the Cuisinar Waffle Maker.
5. Add the mixture to the waffle maker.
6. Bake according to directions.

Serving Suggestions: Serve with maple syrup.

Preparation & Cooking Tips: Use day old bread for this recipe.

Choco Strawberry Waffle

Preparation Time: 10 minutes
Cooking Time: 5 minutes
Servings: 4

Ingredients:

- 1 ½ cups all purpose flour
- 2 teaspoon baking powder
- ½ teaspoon baking soda
- 1 tablespoon sugar
- 3 eggs, beaten
- ¾ cup milk
- ¼ cup vegetable oil
- ¼ cup chocolate syrup
- ¼ cup butter, melted
- ½ cup sour cream
- 1 cup whipping cream
- 2 cups strawberries, sliced

Method:

1. Add flour, baking powder, baking soda and sugar to a bowl. Mix well.
2. In another bowl, whisk together eggs, milk, oil, syrup and butter.
3. Stir in sour cream and whipping cream.
4. Add this mixture to the flour mixture.
5. Fold in strawberries.
6. Prepare waffles in the Cuisinar Waffle Maker as directed.

Serving Suggestions: Top with whipped cream and fresh strawberry slices.

Preparation & Cooking Tips: Use low fat cream.

Mixed Nut Waffle

Preparation Time: 10 minutes
Cooking Time: 5 minutes
Servings: 4

Ingredients:

- 1 ½ cups flour
- 2 teaspoons baking powder
- 1 tablespoon sugar
- ½ teaspoon salt
- ¼ cup cashews, chopped
- ¼ cup almonds, chopped
- 2 tablespoons butter, melted
- 2 eggs, beaten

Method:

1. Put all the ingredients in a bowl.
2. Mix well.
3. Plug the Cuisinar Waffle Maker.
4. Turn knob to shade setting that you like.
5. When the blue light is on, add the mixture to the waffle maker.
6. Close the machine.
7. When blue light turns on, open and serve waffle.

Serving Suggestions: Drizzle with honey.

Preparation & Cooking Tips: You can also add other nuts to the mixture.

Choco Fudge Waffle

Preparation Time: 15 minutes
Cooking Time: 10 minutes
Servings: 6

Ingredients:

- 4 tablespoons butter
- 2 oz. baking chocolate
- 3 eggs, beaten
- 1 cup buttermilk
- 1 teaspoon vanilla extract
- 1 ¼ cups flour
- ½ teaspoon baking powder
- ½ teaspoon baking soda
- 2/3 cup sugar
- Pinch salt
- 3 oz. chocolate chips, chopped

Method:

1. Add butter and baking chocolate to a pan over medium heat.
2. Cook for 5 minutes or until melted.
3. Set aside.
4. In a bowl, combine the remaining ingredients, adding chocolate chips last.
5. Add chocolate mixture and mix well.
6. Prepare waffle in the Cuisinar Waffle Maker as directed.

Serving Suggestions: Drizzle with chocolate syrup.

Preparation & Cooking Tips: Use unsweetened baking chocolate or dark chocolate chips.

Chocolate Waffle with Banana & Caramel

Preparation Time: 15 minutes
Cooking Time: 15 minutes
Servings: 2

Ingredients:

Waffle

- 1 ½ cups baking mix
- 1 cup sugar
- 1/3 cup baking cocoa
- ¾ cup water
- 2 tablespoons vegetable oil
- 2 eggs

Topping

- ¼ cup whipping cream
- ½ cup brown sugar
- 2 tablespoons butter
- ¼ cup corn syrup
- 3 banana, sliced
- 1 teaspoon vanilla

Method:

1. Combine waffle ingredients in a bowl. Mix well.
2. Bake in the Cuisinar Waffle Maker as directed.
3. While waiting, make the topping.
4. Add topping ingredients to a pan over medium heat.
5. Simmer while stirring for 10 minutes.
6. Pour sauce over waffle and serve.

Serving Suggestions: Dust with confectioners' sugar.

Preparation & Cooking Tips: Use light corn syrup.

Cinnamon & Raisin Waffle

Preparation Time: 10 minutes
Cooking Time: 5 minutes
Servings: 4

Ingredients:

- 1 ½ cups baking mix
- 1 cup sugar
- ¾ cup water
- 2 tablespoons vegetable oil
- 2 eggs
- 1 teaspoon ground cinnamon
- 3 tablespoons raisins

Method:

1. Combine all the ingredients in a bowl.
2. Mix well.
3. Turn on the Cuisinar Waffle Maker.
4. Choose shade setting that you like.
5. When the blue light is on, add mixture to the machine.
6. Close and wait for blue light to turn on again before opening.
7. Let cool and serve.

Serving Suggestions: Serve with honey.

Preparation & Cooking Tips: You can also use canola oil instead of vegetable oil.

Apple, Cinnamon & Pumpkin Waffle

Preparation Time: 15 minutes

Cooking Time: 5 minutes

Servings: 6

Ingredients:

- 2 egg whites
- ½ cup pumpkin puree
- ½ cup apple, shredded
- ½ cup applesauce
- 1 cup milk
- 1 cup all-purpose flour
- ½ cup brown sugar
- 1 ½ teaspoons baking powder
- 1 teaspoon cinnamon
- ¼ teaspoon salt
- ¼ teaspoon nutmeg
- 1/8 teaspoon ginger
- 1/8 teaspoon ground cloves

Method:

1. Beat eggs using a hand mixer until fluffy.
2. Add to a bowl.
3. Stir in the rest of the ingredients.
4. Plug the Cuisinar Waffle Maker to begin preheating.
5. Select shade setting preferred.
6. Once blue light is on, add mixture.
7. Seal and wait for blue light to turn on again before opening.
8. Let cool and serve.

Serving Suggestions: Serve with syrup of choice.

Honey Whole Wheat Waffle

Preparation Time: 10 minutes
Cooking Time: 5 minutes
Servings: 8

Ingredients:

- 1 cup all purpose flour
- 1 cup whole wheat flour
- 2 teaspoons baking powder
- 2 teaspoons sugar
- ½ teaspoon salt
- ¼ cup honey
- 3 eggs, beaten
- 1 ½ cups milk
- ¼ cup butter
- 1 teaspoon vanilla

Method:

1. Add dry ingredients to a bowl.
2. Stir in one by one the wet ingredients.
3. Mix well.
4. Prepare waffle according to Cuisinar Waffle Maker instructions.
5. Let cool and serve.

Serving Suggestions: Dust with confectioners' sugar.

Preparation & Cooking Tips: You can also add chopped pecans to the mixture.

Conclusion

The recipes in this cookbook will guide you in details so that you can make tasty waffles without thinking too much and this cookbook will also help save your money and time. Uncover the delicious world of waffles and kick start your new lifestyle! Waffles are not just for breakfast, and once you master these easy basic recipes you can use them in myriad other recipes.

Wait no more!

Go ahead to have these recipes in your hand right now to save you time and effort with the easiest and all kinds of waffle recipes.